Bouki's HONEY

Based on The Creole Folktales

"Compaire Bouki and Compaire Lapin"

Written by: Arthur "Roy" Williams

Designed and Illustrated by: L. Foote

AuthorHouse™
1663 Liberty Drive
Bloomington, IN 47403
www.authorhouse.com
Phone: 833-262-8899

Because of the dynamic nature of the Internet, any web addresses or links contained in this book may have changed since publication and may no longer be valid. The views expressed in this work are solely those of the author and do not necessarily reflect the views of the publisher, and the publisher hereby disclaims any responsibility for them.

Any people depicted in stock imagery provided by Getty Images are models, and such images are being used for illustrative purposes only.
Certain stock imagery © Getty Images.

This book is printed on acid-free paper.

ISBN: 978-1-4343-0467-4 (sc)
ISBN: 978-1-6655-2493-3 (hc)

Library of Congress Control Number: 2007905149

Print information available on the last page.

Published by AuthorHouse 07/13/2021

authorHOUSE

Based on The Creole Folktales

"Compaire Bouki and Compaire Lapin"

Written by: Arthur "Roy" Williams
Designed and Illustrated by: L. Foote

*French Creole Language Advisor:
Herbert Wiltz

Book 1
of the Book Series

Dedicated to my grandchildren —

**Micah Jabari, Dominique Jaleel, Christa Adia
and Bradley Eli Williams**

— Arthur "Roy" Williams

About the Author —

Arthur "Roy" Williams is a native of Southwestern Louisiana. When he was a child, he heard many stories about Bouki and Lapin — usually after eating a hearty meal of cornbread and sweet water, or just sitting around the fireplace during winter months eating homemade popcorn. The elders enjoyed telling these Creole folktales — usually in French Creole — as entertainment. Such tales also helped to forget the troubles of the day.

Even to this day, the colorful tales of Bouki and Lapin are shared at folk life and music festivals. Everyone welcomes the adventures of the tricky rabbit Lapin and the simple-minded donkey Bouki.

Mr. Williams, a retired educator, is the owner of a popular Creole restaurant, "Country Cuisine," which is located in Lafayette, Louisiana, where he resides. He is married to the former Rita Zeno. The couple has two sons, a daughter-in-law, and four grandchildren.

About the Designer & Illustrator —

L. Foote is a Louisiana artist who has had numerous art shows and art exhibits with art associations, restaurants, galleries and museums throughout Louisiana.

Foote's art may also be seen on commissions for churches, radio and television programs, businesses, organizations and numerous Louisiana festivals and events, including: African Diaspora Heritage Week, the Juneteenth Folklife Celebration and the Original Southwest Louisiana Zydeco Music Festival.

About the French Creole Advisor —

Herbert Wiltz learned French Creole at an early age, hearing it spoken by his grandmother and other family members and friends. His interest in languages grew after discovering an aunt's French grammar book.

Wiltz went on to receive a scholarship from Southern University, to major in French (minoring in Spanish). Wiltz received his Master's in French at Atlanta University. He has taught both French and Spanish, and served as an administrator at numerous schools in the Southwestern Louisana area. Currently he is teaching French at Milton Elementary/Middle School in Milton, Louisiana.

A Special Thank You —

From everyone involved with this project, to **Dr. Chris Williams** for his unending dedication to the production and completion of this book.

$\mathcal{B}$ouki, the donkey, woke up early one morning, and headed out to fetch some honey — from a beehive he had found just the day before.

On Bouki's way back home, he met his friend Lapin, the rabbit.

"Comment ça va? How are you, Bouki?" Lapin asked cheerfully.

"Ça va bien — I'm doing well," Bouki replied, trying to hide his bright red honey pot.

Lapin just smiled and suggested that they go to the garden to do some field work.

"Mais, okay," said Bouki. "Le' me go get some more garden tools."

Not wanting to return all the way home, Bouki decided to hide his honey in the nearby church tower — so that Lapin would not find it.

But it just so happened that Lapin followed Bouki and watched him hide the honey in the church tower.

"*Mais, tonnere m'écrase*! Well, I'll be," Lapin said to himself. Then Lapin hurried and scurried back out to the garden, and Bouki never even noticed him.

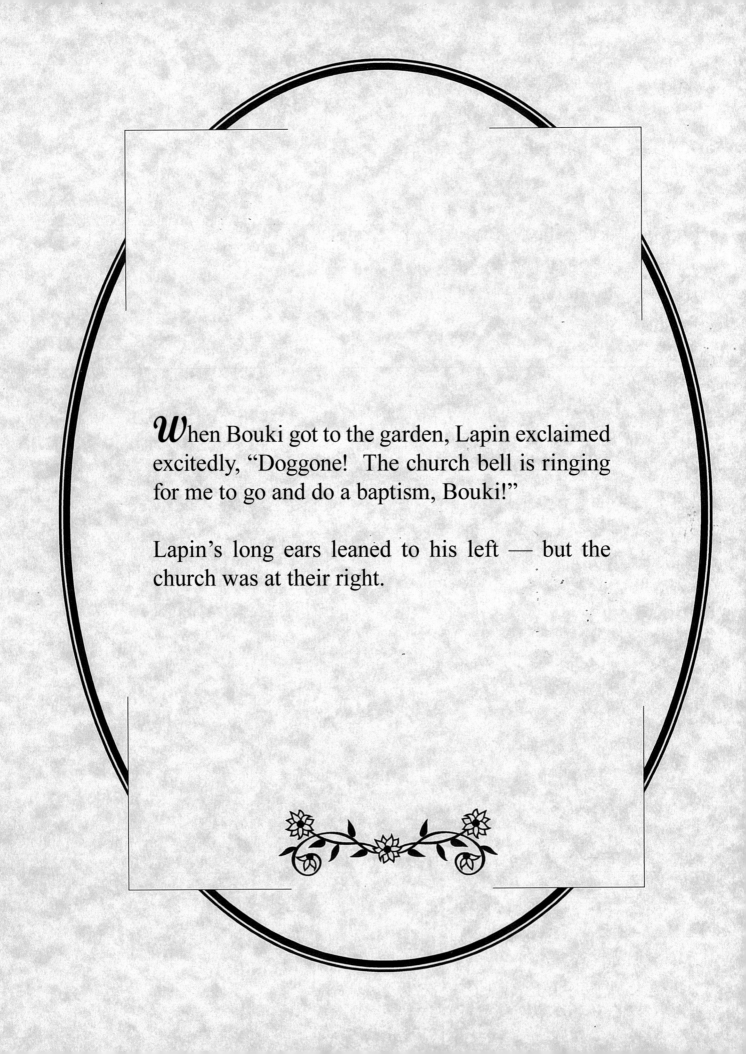

When Bouki got to the garden, Lapin exclaimed excitedly, "Doggone! The church bell is ringing for me to go and do a baptism, Bouki!"

Lapin's long ears leaned to his left — but the church was at their right.

But Bouki never noticed.

"You know you have to go Lapin, because you are an ordained minister," Bouki said, "and baptisms are your duty."

Lapin chuckled to himself, and off he went to the church tower and ate some of Bouki's delicious honey.

*W*hen Lapin returned to the garden, Bouki asked him excitedly, "What name did you baptize *le bébé* —the baby, Lapin???"

"*F*irst Time," Lapin replied, trying to look serious.

$\mathcal{B}$ouki continued to work hard in the garden, but a little while later, Lapin exclaimed, "They are calling me again for a baptism, Bouki!"

"Mais Lapin, I don't hear any church bell ringing," Bouki said. Bouki never noticed that Lapin's long ears were leaning in the wrong direction again — and worried that he might be losing his hearing, Bouki pretended that he could also hear the church bell ringing.

"Oh mais yeah, Lapin. I can hear it now," Bouki told Lapin. "You know I can actually hear better than you can. You better hurry and go because a baptism is your duty."

But once again, Lapin snuck to the church tower to eat some more of Bouki's honey.

Upon Lapin's return, Bouki asked, "Lapin! Lapin! What name did you baptize le bébé — the baby???"

"*Second Time*," replied Lapin, trying not to laugh.

"That's a funny name for a baby — '*Second Time*'," Bouki said.

$\mathcal{T}$ime passed, as Bouki continued to work hard in the garden, and Lapin sat on his furry tail and watched.

Then suddenly Lapin exclaimed, "Bouki! They're calling me *again* for a baptism — but I'm not gonna go because you are doing almost all of the garden work."

"Go," said Bouki. "You don't want to refuse a baptism, Lapin. C'est ton droit — it is your duty."

"No. I'm not going," Lapin said again.

*B*ut Bouki insisted. "You *must* go, Lapin," he said. "*C'est ton droit* — it is your duty."

But once again, Lapin went to the church tower — and *THIS* time, he ate **all** the honey that Bouki had hidden!

When Lapin returned to the garden, Bouki again asked, "So Lapin, what name did you baptize *le bébé* — the baby???"

"*Tout Fini — All Finished*," Lapin replied in Creole and then in English. And then he laughed and laughed.

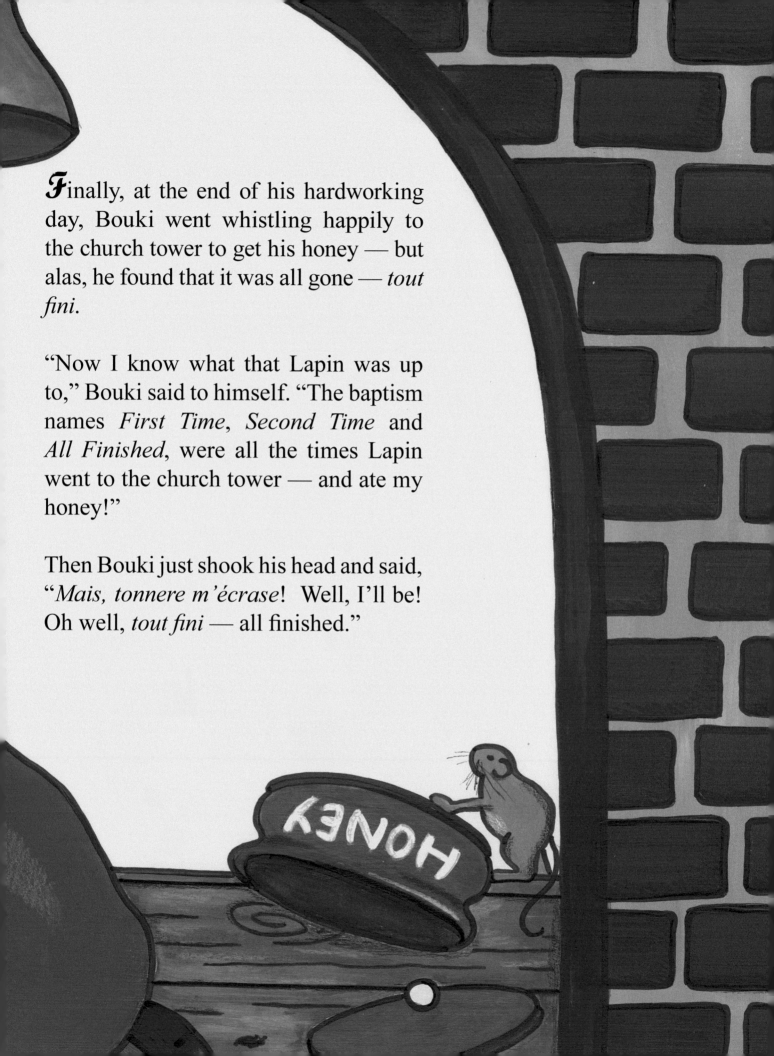

*F*inally, at the end of his hardworking day, Bouki went whistling happily to the church tower to get his honey — but alas, he found that it was all gone — *tout fini.*

"Now I know what that Lapin was up to," Bouki said to himself. "The baptism names *First Time, Second Time* and *All Finished,* were all the times Lapin went to the church tower — and ate my honey!"

Then Bouki just shook his head and said, "*Mais, tonnere m'écrase!* Well, I'll be! Oh well, *tout fini* — all finished."

A Guide to the
French Creole in

"Bouki's Honey"

French Creole	Pronounced	English
1. Lapin	lah-pan	rabbit
2. comment ça va	koh-mo sah va	How are you?
3. ça va bien	sah vah bee an	I'm doing well
4. mais tonnere m'écrase	mayh tone-nair maykras	well, I'll be
5. le bébé	lub beh beh	the baby
6. mais	meh or mayh	but / well
7. C'est ton droit	say tahn dwa	it is your duty / privilege
8. tout fini	too fee nee	all finished
9. Au voir	Oh-vwah	goodbye
10. cher	shair	dear

("r" sound is almost silent)

We hope you enjoy learning these words and expressions

in French Creole —

After you have collected 10 books from the series,
*you and your family should know
about 100 French Creole words / expressions*

C'est bon, cher!!!

About Compaire Bouki and Compaire Lapin

The Creole folktales of Bouki and Lapin have a rich and fascinating history, hundreds of years old. The tales originated from Senegal, Africa, and according to the Louisiana Creole Plantation, *'Laura,'* they were first recorded in the United States — in Laura Plantation's 150-year-old cabins.

Lapin's adventures soon went on to become the popular American tales known as *"Br'er (Brother) Rabbit"* — only *'Compaire Bouki and Compaire Lapin'* have a unique, French Creole 'flavor'. (In French folklore, 'compaire/compair' means brother.)

The name 'Bouki' is a "wolof" word — 'wolof' being both the language and the people of Senegal, Africa — and is said to mean, *"stupid hyena."* Some even say 'Bouki' is a play on words meaning, 'bookish' (something that the character never is).

Bouki has had numerous spellings over the years, including, but probably not limited to "Bouqui, Bouky, Boukee, Bookee and Bookie." In various stories from Louisiana he is pictured as a donkey, a raccoon or a wolf. He was a hyena in the original African folktales.

'Lapin' means *"rabbit"* in French. Thus we have the often humorous tales of 'Lapin' — the clever, trickster rabbit, and 'Bouki', the slow-witted donkey. It is believed that the Senegal slaves brought to Louisiana, told the African-based stories of Lapin and Bouki as 'code' to show the slave 'Lapin' outwitting the plantation owner, 'Bouki', and thereby triumphing over slavery. Indeed, the folktales of Bouki and Lapin, are stories told — with a cupful of Creole humor — about *"determination, overcoming obstacles* and *triumphing over challenging circumstances."*

Today, 'Compaire Bouki and Compaire Lapin' continue to be popular French Creole folktales, passed from one generation to the next…

Be sure to collect all of the

'Bouki and Lapin' titles

from the book series!

Printed in the United States
by Baker & Taylor Publisher Services